The Drop
That Became
The Sea

Yunus Emre

The Drop
That Became
The Sea
Lyric Poems of
Yunus Emre

Translated from the Turkish by
Kabir Helminski and Refik Algan

THRESHOLD BOOKS

SHAMBHALA
Boston & London
2000

SHAMBHALA PUBLICATIONS, INC.
Horticultural Hall
300 Massachusetts Avenue
Boston, Massachusetts 02115
www.shambhala.com

Printed in the United States of America

Distributed in the United States by Random House, Inc.,
and in Canada by Random House of Canada Ltd

LIBRARY OF CONGRESS CATALOGING-IN-PUBLICATION DATA

Yunus Emre, d. 1320?
   [Selections. English. 1989]
   The drop that became the sea : lyric poems of Yunus Emre / translated by
   Kabir Helminski and Refik Algan.
   96 pp.
   ISBN 0-939660-30-x : $8.00
   1. Helminski, Edmund. 1947–   II. Algan, Refik. 1947–   III. Title.
PL248.Y8A24   1989   89-4404
894'.3511—dc19   CIP
BVG 01

Contents

YUNUS EMRE:
An Introduction

When the song-poems of Yunus Emre spread among the rural Anatolian Turks in the fourteenth century, the Turkish language, already rich in idiom and vocal harmony, began to express the deeper nature of the human spirit. An illiterate peasant with a modest vocabulary of perhaps several thousand words gave utterance to the kind of truths that had been the domain of classical Arabic and Persian. A great poet helped his people to say what they could not say before. While many of his contemporaries imitated Persian and Arabic forms and borrowed their vocabularies, Yunus sang in the language of the common man and used simpler poetic forms. No one has ever matched Yunus's handling of the Turkish vernacular and its syllabic meters.

His words to this day express the deepest aspirations of the Turkish people, an independent, undogmatic, humanistic, and mystical race. His songs are quoted by peasants and scholars, shaikhs and diplomats, the old and the young Yunus Emre's work is both the beginning and the highest achievement of a poetic tradition that has spanned seven centuries. No other poet in the Turkish language has greater authority, and Yunus has been called "the most important folk poet in the literature of Islam." (Talat Sait Halman)

If I were to suggest the importance of Yunus Emre within Turkish civilization, I would invoke Francis of Assisi, Blake, and Yeats. Like Francis he was simple and saintly. He loved the natural world and sang songs. Like Blake his songs are full of symbols. And as Blake stood squarely within his own truth and voiced a cry against much that was mechanical and insensitive in his times, Yunus, with gentleness and charm, attacked the spiritless orthodoxy of his day. Finally, like Yeats his lyrics master stanza and line and can appeal to ordinary people, as well as those with literary interests.

Yunus's Times

The world into which Yunus Emre was born was ruled by the Seljuk Turks centered in Konya (Iconium). Konya and the surrounding region of Anatolia had become a haven for many people from Central Asia, who had fled the pillage, destruction, and death worked by the Mongols. Among these people were great scholars and saints, because Central Asia, particularly in the area of Bokhara, Samarkand, and Tashkent, had developed a state of culture to rival any in the world. Two who came from Central Asia were Mevlana Jelaluddin Rumi, the incomparable poet and spiritual master, and Hadji Bektash Veli, the initiator of a popular, rural Sufi order, the Bektashis, with whom Yunus was associated.

The influences of these two men were to profoundly affect the course of history. Rumi, a sophisticated mystical poet, a philosopher of Cosmic Love, drew upon the everyday lives of people to explain the deepest mysteries. Writing in Persian, his greatest influence would be on the educated, cultured urban elite. Hadji Bektash transmitted a similar energy of Love and humanism but to different people: the rural Anatolian peasants, farmers and herders who lived in compact villages across the dry and often mountainous land.

Ahmed Yasawi, another Central Asian Sufi, had been the first to use the Turkish language as a literary medium with his *Hikam*, a book of mystical reflections. But Yunus was to be the poetic flowering of this impulse brought by Hadji Bektash and Ahmed Yasawi. His language would captivate both the rough and the cultivated for centuries to come. His name would become associated with a whole genre of poetry and song, many anonymous imitators would have their work ascribed to him.

A story told about a meeting between Jelaluddin Rumi and Yunus Emre illustrates the difference between the two. Yunus had become acquainted with the six books of Rumi's masterpiece, the Mathnawi, and he was asked what he thought of it. "It's a little long. I would have written it differently."

"Oh, how so?," Jelaluddin asked.

"I would have written: I came from eternity, clothed myself with skin and bones and called myself 'Yunus'."

Yunus's Life

What can we know about the life of Yunus Emre? His year of birth is uncertain and that of his death is speculated to be 1320. Almost everything we suppose about him is drawn from Yunus's songs themselves, although there are stories of his life that are part of an oral tradition.

When Yunus was young a famine overtook Anatolia. His village has been hard hit and one of the few places that was known to have food was the Sufi center of Hadji

Bektash Veli. A Bektashi center would have been a village in itself, since this particular tradition stressed an integration of social, economic, and esoteric activities within the context of communal life.

As the story goes, Yunus was sent by the people of his village to get some grain from Hadji Bektash's tekkye, or spiritual center. The great shaikh, however, knew presentiently of Yunus's approach and told his doorkeeper to greet Yunus and ask him whether he would like grain or "baraka." Yunus, a shepherd boy, had never heard this word "baraka" before, so he asks whether baraka will take up as much space and weigh as much as grain. He is told that baraka will take up very little room, but he remembers that his village has sent him to get grain, and so he holds firmly to his original request. On the way back to his village Yunus is at first very happy, but later he begins to have some doubts about whether he has done the right thing. Hadji Bektash is, after all, a very generous man and no one seemed to resent Yunus's choice. Maybe this baraka is something very valuable like gold. Halfway through his journey, Yunus decides that he has probably made a mistake and should return and inquire again about the baraka. When he returns, however, he is told that his portion of baraka (spiritual power) has been sent to Taptuk Emre, another Bektashi shaikh destined to become Yunus's guide on the Path.

So Yunus himself becomes a pupil in the school of Taptuk Emre, undergoing many practical as well as spiritual tasks. For many years he remains humbly in the service of his shaikh. The Bektashis call their guides "Shahim" or "My King," and they submit themselves body and soul with total love to the shaikh. After this period of service Yunus is one day abruptly called to Taptuk Emre's presence and told that it is time to leave the center and go out into the world to teach.

Yunus, too humble to believe he has anything to teach, yet submissive to his Shaikh's will, bearing only the practical knowledge of a peasant, goes modestly into the world. While crossing a large desert on foot he encounters two other dervish travelers who invite him to travel with them for safety and companionship. After the first day they stop at dusk to have a meal. One of the dervishes offers a prayer and asks that they be given food to eat. No sooner had it been mentioned than a dinner setting appears with fine bread, vegetables and fruit. Yunus is amazed. On the second night they again stop to eat, and the other dervish prays and produces a meal comparable to the first. Again Yunus is amazed but getting nervous. What if he is asked to produce a meal? On the following night, the other dervishes look to Yunus, and one of them asks, "Would you be the one tonight, brother?" And so Yunus prays within himself: "Oh my God, it wasn't *I* who chose to undertake this journey. I was sent. I do not understand prayers like these, but I know that my shaikh is much beloved by You, and so I ask in his name that you don't cause us embarassment."

Almost immediately the food appears, but it is not the kind of dinner that they had eaten on the two previous nights. Instead it is a feast suitable for a king. The other two dervishes are completely surprised. "In whose name did you pray, brother?" But Yunus, gaining some confidence, says, "First you must tell me in whose name you prayed." "Oh, it is no secret. We were taught to pray in the name of a certain dervish Yunus of Taptuk's Tekkye."

The Godization of Man

The mystic humanism of Anatolia attributed Divine qualities to the human being. The true human nature however, is not automatically received but must be developed from its latent condition. The real human being is the product of a process that brings the human being to an awareness of itself as an extension of the Divine Reality. The human being is fundamentally a reflector of the one Creative Power. Spiritual "maturity" takes away the "and" that is in the phrase "God and man." Godliness finds its grounding in the human being who is aware of his connectedness to the Divine Nature.

Yunus Emre is the quintessence of this humanization of God. Yunus's songs are a natural outpouring of his state of being, that which he could not hold back from us. These songs remind us that life is precious, for it is here that we can free ourselves of our bonds and enter the presence of the Friend. It is in life that we can remember death and be more alive.

There is an implicit humility in much of Yunus's work and a love of humanity. He downplayed dogma, rituals, and religious commentaries. He satirized the hypocrisy of the religious establishment but also leveled some of his harshest criticism at himself. Running through these songs is the affirmation that Love is the cause and essence of everything. And Love is the milieu in which we exist, the source of every quality, virtue, and perfection. It is through Love that the Beloved, the Friend, calls us forth, causes our psyche to embrace more and more.

At times Yunus's very identity seems diaphanous, all-embracing, universal. Such an expansion is possible since the Human Being is the drop which can become the ocean.

There are times when the voice behind these words is not an individual human being but the Creative Power Itself.

Sacred Hymns

Yunus's lyrics are sacred songs that would have been sung in Sufi ceremonies and group worship. They would also be sung informally as a social pastime. Much of the beauty of these lyrics comes from a marriage of idiom and meter which no translator could hope to equal in another language. The translator is faced with choosing between the standards of literature and the accessibility of song. Since these translations are meant to be read and to be reasonably faithful to the meaning of Yunus's words, I have chosen literary translation in free verse as a form rather than popular song. It should be remembered, though, that Yunus was not a "lettered" person. He was a pre-literate, an inspired shepherd. For this reason my translation has been guided by a sense of conversational idiom, the spoken word.

Some centuries after Yunus lived, a collection of his songs came into the hands of a certain orthodox and narrow-minded cleric by the name of Mullah Kasim. This Mullah Kasim sat himself down on the bank of a stream and began to read Yunus's lyrics. Reading through song after song, the Mullah could be heard to mutter the word "blasphemy," crumpling that particular page and throwing it into the stream. Unfortunately he had gone through about two-thirds of the collection before he read the line in which Yunus reminds himself, "Speak truly, for one day a Mullah Kasim will judge you."

At that point the Mullah stopped discarding pages. The lyrics that were not cast upon the waters comprise what we know of Yunus's work today. Most of the poems here can be found in the collection of the scholar Golpinarli and are fully accepted as the work of Yunus Emre. Also included are some of the best known and loved songs of Turkish folk tradition, like "The Rivers of Paradise," which are of more questionable origin. It is a convention of this type of lyric to include the author's name in the last stanza. Many songs exist with Yunus' name in the final stanza whose authorship is actually anonymous. I have chosen to include some of these less authoritative selections as well, songs which belong to the Sea which started with the drop we call Yunus.

Kabir Helminski
Putney, Vermont
February, 1989

I.

The Dervish Way

1.

Whoever is given the dervish path
may his posturing cease and may he shine.

May his breath become musk and amber.
May whole cities and homelands
gather fruit from his branches.

May his leaves be healing herbs for the sick.
May much good work be done in his shadow.

May his tears become a clear lake.
May reeds sprout between his toes.

And among all the poets and nightingales
in the Friend's garden,
may Yunus hop like a partridge.

2.

If I told you about a land of love,
friend, would you follow me and come?
In that land are vineyards
that yield a deadly wine—
no glass can hold it.
Would you swallow it as a remedy?

The people there must suffer.
Would you serve the sweetest drink to others
and take the bitter drink yourself?

There are no moons or suns there.
Nothing waxes or wanes.
Would you surrender your plans
and forget about seductions?

Here we're made of water, earth, fire, and air.
Yunus, tell us, is this what you're made of?

3.

Ask those who know,
what's this soul within the flesh?
Reality's own power.
What blood fills these veins?

Thought is an errand boy,
fear a mine of worries.
These sighs are love's clothing.
Who is the Khan on the throne?

Give thanks for His unity.
He created when nothing existed.
And since we are actually nothing,
what are possessions, houses, shops?

God sent us here
to come and see the world.
This world itself is not everlasting.
What are all of Solomon's riches?

Ask Yunus and Taptuk
what the world means to them.
The world won't last.
What are You? What am I?

4.

We entered the house of realization,
we witnessed the body.

The whirling skies, the many-layered earth,
the seventy-thousand veils,
we found in the body.

The night and the day, the planets,
the words inscribed on the Holy Tablets,
the hill that Moses climbed, the Temple,
and Israfil's trumpet, we observed in the body.

Torah, Psalms, Gospel, Quran—
what these books have to say,
we found in the body.

Everybody says these words of Yunus
are true. Truth is wherever you want it.
We found it all within the body.

5.

The drink sent down from Truth,
we drank it, glory be to God.
And we sailed over the Ocean of Power,
glory be to God.

Beyond those hills and oak woods,
beyond those vineyards and gardens,
we passed in health and joy, glory be to God.

We were dry, but we moistened.
We grew wings and became birds,
we married one another and flew,
glory be to God.

To whatever lands we came,
in whatever hearts, in all humanity,
we planted the meanings Taptuk taught us,
glory be to God.

Come here, let's make peace,
let's not be strangers to one another.
We have saddled the horse
and trained it, glory be to God.

We became a trickle that grew into a river.
We took flight and dove into the sea,
and then we overflowed, glory be to God.

We came down to the valley for winter,
we did some good and some bad things.
Now it's spring and we'll return, glory be to God.

We became servants at Taptuk's door.
Poor Yunus, raw and tasteless,
finally got cooked, glory be to God.

6.

Let's say the name of Allah all the time.
Let's see what my Lord does.
Let's travel the Way always.
Let's see what my Lord does.

Just when you least expect it,
suddenly the veil is lifted.
The remedy arrives in time.
Let's see what my Lord does.

What did Yunus do?
What did he do?
He found a straight Path,
held the hand of a guide.
Let's see what my Lord does.

7.

The mature ones are a sea.
A lover is needed to take the plunge,
a diver to bring up a pearl.

When you have brought
the pearl to the surface,
a jeweler is needed to know its worth.

Stay on the road until you arrive.
Be speechless. Don't become a salesman.
Find an 'Ali to follow.

Muhammed knew Truth in himself.
Truth is present everywhere.
You only need eyes to see it.

Ask your daily sustenance from Truth,
the only Apportioner.* Find someone
who is master of his ego.

The lovers asked me to sing.
Someone without greed is needed
to complete what is started.

Sufi, who are you kidding?
Can anyone but Truth
satisfy a human need?

Truth's place is in the heart.
There's a verse in the *Quran*—In the soul
love has a tower higher than the throne of Creation.

* see: *Quran*: Sura XLIII, 32...

I've gone crazy on this Way.
I can't tell day from night.
The arrow of Love has pierced my heart.

Come, poor Yunus, come,
hold the hands of the mature.
In their humility is a cure.

8.

Our laws are different from other laws.
Our religion is like no other.

It is different from the seventy-two sects.
We are guided by different signs,
in this world and hereafter.

Without the cleansing of visible waters,
without any movement of hands, feet, or head —
we worship.

Whether at the Kaaba*, in the mosque, or in ritual prayer,
everyone carries their own disease.

Which labels refer to whom, no one really knows.
Tomorrow it will be clear who abandoned the religion.

Yunus, renew your soul, be remembered as a friend,
Know this power. Listen with the ears of love.

* Kaaba: An ancient black cube in Mecca and the focal point
ofthe Islamic Pilgrimage or Hajj.

9.

Let the deaf listen to the mute.
A soul is needed to understand them both.

Without listening we understood.
Without understanding we carried it out.

On this Way, the seeker's wealth is poverty.

We loved, we became lovers.
We were loved, we became the beloved.
When all is perishing moment by moment
who has time to be bored?

God divided His people into Seventy-two languages
and borders arose.

But poor Yunus fills the earth and sky,
and under every stone hides a Moses.

10.

I haven't come here to settle down.
I've come here to depart.
I am a merchant with lots of goods,
selling to whoever will buy.
I didn't come to create any problems,
I'm only here to love.
A Heart makes a good home for the Friend.
I've come to build some hearts.
I'm a little drunk from this Friendship—
Any lover would know the shape I'm in.
I've come to exchange my twoness,
to disappear in One.
He is my teacher. I am His servant.
I am a nightingale in His garden.
I've come to the Teacher's garden
to be happy and die singing.
They say "Souls which know each other here,
know each other there."
I've come to know a Teacher
and to show myself as I am.

11.

A single word can brighten the face
of one who knows the value of words.
Ripened in silence, a single word
acquires a great energy for work.

War is cut short by a word,
and a word heals the wounds,
and there's a word that changes
poison into butter and honey.

Let a word mature inside yourself.
Withhold the unripened thought.
Come and understand the kind of word
that reduces money and riches to dust.

Know when to speak a word
and when not to speak at all.
A single word turns a universe of hell
into eight paradises.

Follow the Way. Don't be fooled
by what you already know. Be watchful.
Reflect before you speak.
A foolish mouth can brand your soul.

Yunus, say one last thing
about the power of words—
Only the word "I"
divides me from God.

12.

Dervishood tells me, you cannot become a dervish.
So what can I tell you? You cannot become a dervish.

A dervish needs a wounded heart and eyes full of tears.
He needs to be as easy going as a sheep.
You can't be a dervish.

He must be without hands when someone hits him.
He must be tongueless when cursed.
A dervish needs to be without any desire.
You can't be a dervish.

You make a lot of sounds with your tongue, meaningful things.
You get angry about this and that.
You can't be a dervish.

If it were all right to be angry on this path,
Muhammed himself would have gotten angry.
Because of your anger, you can't be a dervish.

Unless you find a real path, unless you find a guide,
unless Truth grants you your portion,
you can't be a dervish.

Therefore, dervish Yunus, come,
dive into the ocean now and then.
Unless you dive in the ocean, you cannot be a dervish.

II.

The Way of Love

13.

To be in love with love is to gain a soul,
to sit on the throne of hearts.

To love the world is to be afflicted.
Later the secrets start to make sense.

Don't be a bramble,
become the rose. Let your maturity unfold.
The brambles will only burn.

Prayer was created by God so man could ask for help.
It's too bad if you haven't learned to ask.

Accept the breath of those who are mature—
let it become your divining rod.
If you obey your self, things turn out wrong.

Renouncing the world is the beginning of worship.
If you are a believer, believe this.

Respect your parents and ancestry,
and you will have fine green clothes of your own.

If you earn the complaints of neighbors,
You'll stay in Hell forever.

Yunus heard these words from the masters.
If you need this advice, take it.

They say one who is received by a heart
becomes more beautiful.

14.

True speech is the fruit of not speaking.
Too much talking clouds the heart.

If you want to clear the heart,
say this much, the essence of all talking:

Speak truly. God speaks through words truly spoken.
Falsity ends in pain.

Unless you witness all of creation in a single glance,
you're in sin even with all your religion.

The explanation of the Law is this:
The Law is a ship. Truth is her ocean.

No matter how strong the wood,
the sea can smash the ship.

The secret is this:
A "saint" of religion may in reality be an unbeliever.

We will master this science and read this book of love.
God instructs. Love is His school.

Since the glance of the saints fell on poor Yunus
nothing has been a misfortune.

15.

Leave appearances. Come to essence and meaning.
Don't dwell in images or you'll never mature.

The Way is amazing but don't be deceived.
Let it be a wonder to see the Friend's face.

Dress yourself in love. Set out on the Way to the Friend.
Persevere and you'll have so much to see.

From here to the city of Love three hundred oceans you'll trav
and after crossing them seven hells.

Let yourself burn up, burn to ashes in each one,
until nothing's left of your body, except a very different one.

The city of Reality has seven doors, and over a gate the words
Come in and know the power of your Lord.

At the first door sits someone with a moon-like glow,
secure, without blemish, who knows what it is to be poor.

At the second door are two lions who've scared many away.
At the third door are three dragons—but don't turn back.

At the fourth door are four great saints.
You carry this word as a sign and evidence for admission.

At the fifth door are five monks
with much to sell, but you are to buy nothing.

At the sixth door sits a virgin,
radiant as the moon, but don't go to her,

because if you go to her and take her
and satisfy yourself, you'll fall short of your goal.

At the seventh door, seven great men of God
will say to you: You're safe,
come inside and meet the Friend.

These words I've spoken are not outside the body.
If you meditate you'll find them too.

Yunus speaks every word from the One Word.
If it is this ore you seek, you'll find it in humbleness.

16.

That by which our hearts are held,
whole worlds love it too.
I can't deny the truth—
many ways lead to the One.

Those whom the Beloved loves,
we must also love.
If someone is a friend to the Friend,
how can we afford not to be friends?

If you would be a lover,
befriend him who loves your Friend;
and if you cannot,
don't call yourself a friend of mine.

Whomever you tend to despise,
hold dear instead.
Don't belittle others, respect them.
This is where the path leads.

If your heart is filled with love,
your way is sacrifice.
Through sacrifice you will find your place
in the ranks of Love.

Hearts which truly love the Truth,
Truth will open a door wide.
Dismantle the house of selfishness.
Put away your self-regard.

High and low, enemy, neighbor,
the Friend serves them all.
Whoever wants to spread this word
must first go out of his home.

This counsel that Yunus gives
is like buried gold.
Those who love the Friend
find peace in both worlds.

17.

Oh Friend, when I began to love You,
my intellect went and left me.
I gazed at the rivers. I dove into the seas.

But a spark of Love's fire
can make the seas boil.
I fell in, caught fire, and burned.

A soul in love is free of worries.
With love all problems left me.
With love I became happy.

When the nightingale saw the face
of the red rose, it fell in love.
I saw the faces of those who matured,
and became a nightingale.

I was a dead tree fallen onto the path.
When a master threw me a glance
and brought me to life.

Yunus, if you are a true lover,
humble yourself.
Humility was chosen by them all.

18.

How strange I feel under the hand of this love.
I can't see my way, under the hand of this love.

Once I was the crown of the universe.
Now I'm dirt to walk on, under the hand of this love.

Like a lonely nightingale I call.
Blood streams from my eyes, under the hand of this love.

My face, like an autumn leaf, will glow,
darken and die, under the hand of this love.

On the Final Day with my collar torn
let me weep, under the hand of this love.

What can I do when I'm so far from Union?
My back is bent, under the hand of this love.

Yunus, you pray for Taptuk so much.
Don't ask "What shall I do?" under the hand of this love.

19.

What sweet news of love shall I deliver?
Let me speak to those who will listen, one by one.

At first, before earth or sky existed,
without beginning, there was the ground of love,
an infinite beginning,
able to bring anything into existence.

Those who gathered at this beginning
saw the face of the Friend
and became the souls of lovers.
Ask them for news of love.

Don't compare anything to love,
it's not possible.
Nothing substitutes for love
in this world or the next.

Be careful, the news of love is a trust.
Be careful not to speak to just anyone.

Among jewellers there's an unspoken rule:
don't show a pearl to someone who won't know
          its worth.

Yunus's mind was so filled with love,
he couldn't hide his pain.
Love spoke through him.
He didn't choose to.

20.

Beloved, Your love pierces stone.
I lost head and soul in this love.

I fill Your night and day with my sorrow.
You've become a friend of my love.

Someone who worries only about You
is saved from many fears.

The heart that falls into Your love, burns and burns.
The one who gives himself to You,
gives up everything else.

Worldliness looks like a poison.
Someone who lives with a vision of the End
passes up poisons.

Someone who is sane doesn't do the Work for wages.
He doesn't become charmed by houries,
he passes up their looks.

A real lover gives his soul to Your house.
Thousands sacrificed their souls just to talk with You.

For the wise this world is a dream.
Someone who gives himself to You,
goes beyond dreams.

Yunus's heart and eyes are filled with a love of Truth.
In good conversation distinctions blur
between stranger and friend.

21.

My soul,
the way of the masters
is thinner than the thinnest.
What blocked Solomon's way was an ant.

Night and day the lover's
tears never end,
tears of blood,
remembering the Beloved.

"The lover is outcast and idle,"
they used to tell me.
It's true.
It happened to me.

I tried to make sense of the Four Books*,
until love arrived,
and it all became a single syllable.

You who claim to be dervishes
and to never do what God forbids—
the only time you're free of sin
is when you're in His hands.

Two people were talking.
One said, "I wish I could see this Yunus."
"I've seen him," the other says,
"He's just another old lover."

* *Torah, Psalms, Gospel, Quran,* considered by Islamic
tradition to be four Divinely revealed books.

22.

Hey friends, whoever swore off love?
What falling star ever set fire to the ocean?

Beloved, the fire of Your love
set the ocean of my heart aflame.
Folks think it's strange how it boils
and miracles come to the surface.

A hundred thousand like Jesus and Moses
wander aimlessly in Your love.
Folks think it strange that the crocodile of love
swallowed me too!

Let the slave learn to swim
before entering the ocean.
The sea of love is bottomless,
don't be surprised when you go down.

An untrained eye mistakes a pearl for a bead
and sells it for almost nothing.
Whoever doesn't see His Face here openly,
tomorrow, wanders around aimless and
            unaware.

Yunus says, "I serve a Master.
Our Taptuk has the Face of the Friend."
If this is hard to believe,
do whatever else you can.

23.

Do you know, my friends, where the real saints are?
Wherever I look, wherever I want them, they're there.

My words bounce off the loveless like an echo from stone.
Do you know, whoever hasn't got at least an atom of love,
lives in a wilderness?

Don't be a liar, don't lie to love.
Whoever lies here, earns a sentence in the other world.

Oh, you unaware of Yourself,
you don't understand the meaning of words,
if you desire the realness of Truth,
here it is in knowledge and in the *Quran*:

If Allah says, "He is Mine,"
Allah keeps giving the realness of Love.
Whoever has an atom of Love,
has the realness of God within.

Many people tell Yunus,
"You're too old to be a lover,"
but this love is so new and fresh.

24.

I wasn't sober until
I drank the wine of Love.
I didn't know myself
until I met a master.

Is your own knowledge enough
to bring you where you have to go?
You won't reach Allah, you'll be stuck,
unless you take a hand.

If religion and faith are what you want,
work hard and be righteous in this life.
But unless you finish it today,
you'll have the same task in the next world.

A nightingale falls in love with the Rose.
The whole love affair begins
with just one look from God.
A true word ripens within.

It was easy to speak
when my heart was in submission.
Is a lover ever valued for his words
unless he also delivers the goods?

To understand poor Yunus's words,
you have to love very much.
It's like the language of birds—
what can you do but sing?

25.

The moment this sweetheart caught my eye
she washed away my thoughts
and became my heart's companion.

My heart is Her slave. My soul, Her slave.
They struggle over who will be with Her.

But I know that I hold the power over them.
No one ever told me, but She became my happiness.

Wherever I look it's Her that I see.
Even in Winter, Her Spring surrounds me.

I'm no Khidr or Elias,
and sometimes I've made a mess of things;
yet however little I ate and drank, I was well fed.

The whole universe has this Affection inside.
Without this deep Love, faith hardens.

If the fire of Your Love touches anyone, well...
it touched Yunus and opened him to the universe.

*In this poem I have chosen to translate the pronouns as
feminine. The Turkish does not specify gender.*

III.

Necessary Lessons

26.

Wisdom comes from knowing wisdom.
Wisdom means knowing oneself.

If you do not know yourself,
what is the point of reading books?

The point of reading is to know something real.
Since you have read and do not know it,
reading is useless.

Don't say, "I've read, I've learned."
Don't say, "I've worshipped a lot."

If you don't accept the Perfect Man,
all other works are futile.

The meaning of the Four Books is clear and complete.
It shows itself in the first letter, aleph.

If you don't know what aleph is,
what do you know of reading?

You recite every syllable of the alphabet.
You say "Aleph," but how little it means.

Yunus Emre says:
"Hey Hoja, you've made a thousand pilgrimages
but never been welcomed by a single heart."

27.

If you've broken a single heart,
the prayers you make aren't accepted.

The seventy-two peoples of the world
could not wash your hands and face.

So many masters have come and gone.
They migrated. Their ancient lands remain.

They opened their wings and flew to Reality,*
not as geese but as eagles.

A way is true if it's straight.
An eye is that which can see the Real.

And doing good even once is no small thing.
It can return a thousandfold.

Yunus combines words
as if mixing honey into butter.

He's in business among people,
with goods of the highest worth.

* *Al-Haqq*, God, Reality.

28.

Those who became complete
didn't live this life in hypocrisy,
didn't learn the meaning of things
by reading commentaries.

Reality is an ocean; the Law is a ship.
Many have never left the ship,
never jumped into the sea.

They might have come to Worship
but they stopped at rituals.
They never knew or entered the Inside.

Those who think the Four Books
were meant to be talked about,
who have only read explanations
and never entered meaning,
are really in sin.

Yunus means "true friend"
for one whose journey has begun.
Until we transform our Names,
we haven't found the Way.

29.

I am a Sufi in the eyes of the people.
I go around with prayer beads in hand.
My tongue speaks of knowledge
my heart doesn't accept.

I wear a diploma around my neck,
and yet my prayers aren't real.
Worries occupy my mind
and I can't keep my eyes on the Way.

My speaking of knowledge is a kind of lie.
I can't be modest, pride never leaves my heart.

Although I look like a dervish,
I have no patience at all
and I am full of doubts.
Whatever goes in my ears
never reaches the inside.

Those who see me kiss my hand,
they look at my jacket and hat.
They think I am free from sin.

Outwardly I lecture and lead prayers;
inside, in my heart's bazaar
are things even a sly man
wouldn't dream of in a thousand years.

Yunus, put your need in front of Allah.
He is Generous,
He does not do what you do.

30.

Before you're able to give your soul,
you want the Beloved.

Before you discard the rope of doubt,
you want faith.

You repeat, "He who knows himself, knows his Lord."*
But you haven't known and you want to surpass the angels.

You're a child who wants to jump on a horse
and ride into the game without a polo stick.

You don't know you're a pearl within mother-of-pearl.
Without first ruling Egypt, you want the land of Canaan.

Yunus, endure every trouble as Job did.
Don't take the remedy before the pain.

A saying of Muhammed's, peace and blessings upon him.

31.

Sorrowful one, why do you go around in tears?
If my Lord causes me to weep,
surely He will make me laugh some day.

So many of the sorrowful landed here,
then migrated back.
If my lord causes me to weep,
surely He will make me laugh some day.

This suffering is my dearest companion.
When my sighs and tears rise up,
His gifts and kindness are the cause.
If my Lord causes you to weep,
surely He will make you laugh some day.

All the while, turn your face toward the Truth;
all the while, remember His name.
He gives grief to those He favors.
If my Lord cause you to weep,
surely He will make you laugh some day.

Don't leave this poor head of yours in love,
or bloody tears will flow.
He is generous, He even makes repairs.
If my Lord causes you to weep,
surely He will make you laugh some day.

Yunus, so many states before your eyes,
so many places to stop.
Stop and call your Lord night and day.

If my Lord causes you to weep,
surely He will make you laugh some day.

32.

Don't advise those who aren't in love.
The unloving, like animals, can't understand.

Don't distance yourself from the wise,
but avoid the shallow.
The ungiving disappoint God.
They cannot see His face.

Don't waste time on drab pigeons
who consort with moles,
who avoid the deep-diving loon.

Falcon and King, each praises the other.
Even a weak falcon is a falcon still.

And if you wash some dark stone for fifty years,
you won't really transform it.

The hidden sun, Muhammed, changed appearance.
Some say he died. He never does.

Yunus, don't be stupid, mix with the mature.
A fool who talks of spiritual things is still a fool.

IV.

Presence and Unity

33.

Those who learned to be truly human
found everything in being humble.
While those who looked proudly from above,
were pushed down the stairs.
A heart that must always feel superior
will one day lose its way.
What should be within, leaks out.

The old man with the white beard
never sees the state he's in.
He needn't waste money on making the Hajj,
if he's broken someone's heart.

The heart is the seat of God,
where God is aware.
You won't find happiness
in either world, if you break a heart.

The deaf man doesn't hear,
the blind man mistakes day for night.
Yet the universe is filled with light.
We've seen how those who came later moved on.

Whatever you think of yourself,
think the same of others.
This is the meaning of the Four Books,
if they have one.

May Yunus not stray from the path,
nor get on his high horse.
May the grave and the Judgement be no concern,
if what he loves is the face of God.

34.

Whatever I say, You are the subject.
Wherever I go, every impulse is toward You.

It's true, those who don't love You are soul-less dolls,
but the living need a Beloved like You.

You've veiled Yourself from the whole universe.
At a single sight of You it would perish.

Giants and elves, humans, angelic powers,
all beings are in love with You.

The seraphim and maidens of paradise crowd around You
and can't bear to leave Your presence.

From Your hand poison is a delicious drink.
My soul is healed by anything You do.

When I eat something sweet without You, it's bitter.
You are the soul's taste, what else could I want?

If my soul suffered a hundred wounds,
my joy would not decrease.
This love washes everything clean.

Yunus is just one atom of it. This planet,
this whole universe is born from a taste of love.

35.

Soul of my soul,
Without You I have no work to do.
If You are absent from Paradise,
I don't need to go there.
If I look, all I see is You.
If I speak, I speak of You.
There is no better prey
than You whom I secretly watch.
Because I forgot myself,
because I went to You,
in any conversation, in every state,
I haven't got a moment's rest.
You can kill me seventy times,
and like St. George, I'll resurrect,
and crawl back unashamed.

Show Your face to Yunus.
He loves You and has no other.

36.

I am a fatherless pearl unrecognized by the sea.
I am the drop that contains the ocean.

Its waves are amazing. It's beautiful to be a sea
hidden within an infinite drop.

When Majnun spoke Layla's name,
he broke the meter of his poem.
I was both Layla and Majnun who adored her.

Mansur* did not speak idly of Unity.
He was not kidding when he said, "I am Truth."

In this world of many,
You are Joseph and I am Jacob.
In the universe of Unity,
there is neither Joseph nor Canaan.

That my name is Yunus
is a problem in this material world.
But if you ask my real name,
it is the Power behind all powers.

*Mansur al-Hallaj (d. 922), a great Sufi martyred for his
ecstatic utterance.

37.

My love for You goes deeper than my own soul.
My way amounts to this:
I don't say I'm inside of myself. I'm not.
The I within me is deeper than myself.

Anywhere I look, it's filled with You.
Where can I put You if You're already inside.
You are Beauty without features,
something deeper than any signs.

Don't ask me about myself. I'm not inside.
My body walks. I'm clothed, yet empty.
I can't lay a hand on the One who took me from myself.
You can't go over the head of the Boss.

Some people get their share of revelations,
and some people go deeper than this.
In the beautiful light of His face
is a fire brighter than the light of day.

What a suffering it is
that's deeper than any remedy.
The Law and the Brotherhood are paths.
Truth and Wisdom are still deeper.

They say Solomon knew the language of birds.
Within Solomon is a deeper Solomon.
I've forgotten religion and piety.
What if there's a doctrine deeper than religion?

The works of those who leave the faith
are blasphemy. What about a blasphemy
that goes deeper than faith?
Yunus chanced to meet a Friend
who showed him a door inside.

38.

I have found the soul of souls.
Let this soul of mine be taken.

I've forgotten gain and loss.
Let this shop of mine be plundered.

I've passed beyond my very self.
I've removed the veils before me.

I am together with the Friend.
Let these doubts of mine fall away.

My own ego abandoned me.
The Friend took everything I had.

Those who give and take are friends.
Let this language of mine be jumbled.

I cut all ties and went to the Friend.
I fell in with God. Let my poems be scattered.

I became tired of twoness
and ate at the table of Oneness.

I drank the wine of suffering.
Let all my remedies be thrown out.

Since this journey of Being began,
the Friend has rushed to meet us.

Light has filled the ruins of this heart.
Let this universe of mine be shattered.

I have passed up dreams.
I have tired of summers and winters.

I have found the Gardener of flowers.
Let this garden of mine be dug up.

Yunus, you say it well,
smooth as honey.

I have found the honey of honeys.
Let this hive of mine be given away.

39.

I am before and I am after.
I am the life of many lives.
I am Khidr when he appears
to those who have lost their way.

I am the secret found
in settling down to work.
When I hide myself within a heart,
the blind do not need eyes to see me.

The One who causes particles to collide
at the moment of "Be,"*
the One whose glance constructs a world,
the One through whom the table is set,
I am the guardian of every love.

I've made the fields flat
and I've built the mountains.
I put the skies above you.
I sustain all things.

I am the faith of lovers.
I am Islam and I am blasphemy.

The One who gives life and also gives order,
the One who correctly wrote the Four Books,
the One putting black marks
on white sheets of paper,
and the *Quran*—I am.

The one who is united with the Friend
and does what the Friend says,
the Creator of possessions,
Who sets up the world,
I am the Gardener.

The One who carried Hamza over Mount Kaf**,
The One who untied his hands and feet.
That poisonous snake behind the Simurgh
and Kaf, are Me.

This is not Yunus speaking.
but his very Self.
Not to believe this would be blasphemy.
The First, the Last, the Present, I am.

*The moment when God said "BE," and it was.

** Mount Kaf: Literally, the Caucasus Mountains; the cosmic
mountain and the home of the Simurgh, a Divine bird who
was the goal in Attar's Conference of the Birds.

40.

Love is my sect and religion.
When my eyes saw the face of the Friend,
all sorrows became joys.

Here, my King,
I give myself to You.
From beginning to end
all my treasure and richness is You.

The source of this mind and soul,
the origin of space
are with You.
You are the end and everything between.
I can only go toward You.

My way is from You to You.
My tongue speaks of You within You.
And yet my hand can't touch You.
This knowledge amazes me.

I can no longer call myself "I".
I can't call anybody "you" anymore.
I can't say this one is a servant
and that one is a king.
It doesn't make any sense.

Since I found the love of the friend
this world and the next world are one.
If you ask about the infinite beginning
and the infinite end,
they are my night and day.

No longer do I mourn
or cloud my heart,
because truth's voice is heard,
and I'm at my own wedding.

Don't let me wander from Your love,
don't let me leave Your door,
and if I lose myself
let me find myself with You.

The Friend sent me here.
Go and see the world, he said.
I have come and seen
how beautifully it's arranged.
But those who love You don't stay here.

He tells His servants,
Tomorrow I will give you paradise.
That tomorrow is my today.

Who else knows this wisdom and this pain?
And if it is ever known,
it cannot be said.
I turn my face to You.

You are the soul and the universe,
the secret treasure.
All gain and loss is from You.
My acts are no longer my own.

Yunus turns his face to You
forgetting himself.
He speaks every word to You.
It is You who makes him speak

41.

Truth gave me a heart bewildered
before a syllable is spoken.
There comes a moment of happiness,
then one of weeping.
The next moment like winter—long and dark,
the next like a birth—
flower gardens and fine vineyards appear.
A moment comes when he can't speak,
he can't explain a thing!
In another moment pearls fall from his tongue,
remedies for those who suffer.
In another moment he rises to the heights,
in the next he's beneath the earth.
In one moment he's a drop,
in another he's boiled over into an ocean.
One moment he remains in the dark,
he can't know anything;
in the next he dives into a sea of wisdom.
He becomes a Galen, a Luqman.
One moment he becomes a giant or sprite
living in some ruins.
In the next he's flying with Belkis,
he's a sultan of men and jinns.
One moment he enters the mosque
and puts his face to the floor;
the next he's going to church,
reading the Gospel and becoming a monk.
A moment comes when like Jesus
he raises the dead.
A moment comes when he enters the house of pride
and becomes another Pharoah or Hamam.
One moment he's Gabriel
bestowing abundantly to every gathering,
next moment he's lost,
and poor Yunus stands astonished.

42.

The rivers of paradise flow, chanting Allah, Allah.
The nightingales of Islam are perched all around,
singing, Allah, Allah.

The branches of the Tuba tree wave,
each heart and tongue reciting the Quran.
In the rose garden of Paradise, the fragrance of Allah.

Food and drink spread out for you by angels.
The Prophet Idris sewing your astral garments,
chanting, Allah, Allah.

These strolling virgins of Paradise,
their words are musk and amber.
Their faces are brighter than the moon,
singing Allah, Allah.

You fall in love with Truth and begin to cry,
You become holy light both inside and out,
singing Allah, Allah.

Whatever you desire, ask it of Truth.
Be a guide on the straight path.
The nightingale has fallen in love with the rose,
singing Allah.

The doors of the heavens opened,
and the doors of eight paradises,
all singing Allah, Allah.

Rizwan* opens the doors dressed in astral clothes.
Those who drink the wine of Kevser**,
become content and chant, Allah, Allah.

* *Rizwan:* the gatekeeper of Paradise.
** *Kevser:* the spring of Paradise.

Dervish Yunus, go to your lover now,
don't delay another day.
Tomorrow you'll enter the court of Truth,
singing Allah, Allah.

v.

Life and Death

43.

The inner man knows no worries on this path.
The inner heart does not know death.

Bodies perish, but not the soul. Those who are gone
        don't return.
Bodies are for dying. That's not what a soul is for.

The heart will never find the pearl it seeks,
even in a thousand years, unless it's given.

Be careful, your Beloved's heart is easily broken.
Such fine crystal once shattered is never restored.

And unless you put your cup to the fountain,
even in a thousand years it won't be filled.

Both Khidr* and Elias drank the water of life.
These days they are not dead.

The world was made for the sake of the Prophet and
        his friendship.
Those who come to this world do not remain.

Yunus, today while you have eyes to see,
        do what you must.
Those who attain do not come back.

* Khidr in Islamic tradition is an immortal who may appear in
human form to give help and guidance to those in need.

44.

One day I had taken a walk
and came upon a tree of great height.
I said to this slim beauty,
"Tell me a few of your secrets.
What's the meaning of stretching so tall
in such a temporary world?
Come back among the humble again.
You embellish your beauty endlessly,
but why not take some pains for Truth instead?
Find your heart's real need."

The tree will age, its time will pass.
A bird will perch on a branch,
and one day it will seem
there was no bird at all.
One day your end will come,
your great length will fall to earth.
Your branches will be thrown in the fire
and the pots will boil on red hot iron.

Yunus, you are only one,
and yet you have a hundred thousand faults.
Having reflected on a stiff tree's fate,
think of your own.

45.

The Truth fills the world,
but to whom is Truth known?
You ask so much of It,
but It isn't separate from yourself.

You believe in the world,
you claim your daily bread as your own.
How long will you keep up your lie?
You know it's not like that.

It's a long way to the other world.
Be honest with yourself
through all the separation and painful yearning.
Those who attain do not return.

Those who come to the world will
one by one drink the juice of death.
This world is just a bridge
although the young wouldn't guess it.

Come, let's get to know each other
and make our work easier.
Let's love, let's be loved.
No one inherits this world.

Yunus, if you can understand,
if you can hear the meaning,
find a little happiness.
No one's here forever.

46.

Oh disciple of love, open your eyes,
look to the face of the land.
See these subtle plants, how their flowering passes.

With such care they grow toward the Friend—
ask them what goal they have in mind.

Each flower has a thousand ways it flirts with Truth.
Every bird with its song is remembering the Ruler.

They praise His Ability, His Presence in every detail,
yes, and as they see the shortness of life, they pale.

Each day their color changes,
until they fall to the ground.
This is a teaching for the wise to understand.

Your coming doesn't lead anywhere.
Your laughter isn't funny.
Your only destination is death,
if you haven't learned to love.

Yunus, forget about talking,
take your hand off your self. What can you do?
Not a single thing, good or bad, is apart from God.

47.

If you need to be warned, come, look at these graves.
Even a stone would soften after seeing them.

And those with great riches, see to what end they came,
wrapped in simple cloth, a shirt without sleeves.

Where are those who used to say "These riches are mine,"
who weren't satisfied merely with a fine house.

Now they're covered with stone.

They never were at home in God's house.
They neglected the rules, the worship.
They never learned to serve. Now their time is passed.

Here are those who talked so well,
those with sun-tanned faces.
They have died and disappeared.

Once these were the bosses many worked for.
Come and tell me now—which is which?

There's neither a door to enter nor food to eat.
There's no light to see. Daylight is now darkness.

Yunus, all you call your own you'll leave behind.
Your possessions will abandon you.

48.

Put the world and its adornments
aside, the world which weighs
less than a dream or a breeze.

Do you expect it to be faithful?
It's just waiting to run away.

Don't wish for things
as brief as these,
things even the Sultan can't hold on to.

We took our worries with us,
those imaginary companions,
when we could have been with the Friend.

Balance the books yourself,
before someone does it for you.

Kill your compulsive self,
lay it on the stone slab for washing,
so that before death surprises you,
you'll be in the right hands.

Whoever asks you what you believe in,
kiss their hands and feet,
show them the answer.

Yunus, a straight way seems right for you.
Join with Truth now, resurrect with Truth.

49.

Whatever separates you from the Truth,
throw it away, it will vanish anyhow.
Why do you feed this flesh?
In the grave worms and birds will feast on it,
and it will vanish too.

Open your eyes and look at someone who has died.
The beard and hair fall off.
Snakes and centipedes come hungry, feed themselves,
and leave contented.

Those who are greater than us,
those with courtesy and right action,
say "This is the story," and leave.

"Take your hand away from unfair gains,
and hold your gossiping tongue,
before Azrael* comes and closes the shop."

The moment of death comes and the head dries,
old age reaches its end very soon.
Mountains and rocks are flattened,
the sky is rolled up and the earth disappears.**

The soul will face its Day of Reckoning
and so work hard.
The one who worships at dawn,
goes to the House of God matured.

"Yunus, the poor one" will die,
his grave will fill with holy light.
"Faith" will be his comrade
when he goes like a lion to the next world.

*Azrael: Angel of Death.
**An allusion to Quran, Surah XXI, 104.

50.

This King, this King, He keeps on doing His work.
The world is His orchard.
He keeps on sending pain to the one He loves.

Don't do wrong,
the moment of death is closer to you than yourself.
It has made its home in our own roots and origins,
It demolishes us all.

In a single moment you will reach there,
so work hard here.
The soul is not here forever,
it wanders around for a few days in the flesh.

A Questioner comes, tears back the earth,
and asks, "Who is your God?"
And this soul of mine hears him
and my bones keep on aching.

Those who accept God's Unity,
those who sacrifice their souls for God,
these souls are not dead,
they're swimming in the waters of Love.

I have seen—those who attained flew away.
They drank from the full cup of Love.
Their whims are tolerated at the level of Truth,
Their heads are bowed.

Yunus, if you are the servant of the wise,
don't forget your death.
So many of the attained have come and gone,
now our turn has come.

51.

My life came and went
like the wind, between the opening
and closing of an eye.
As Truth is my witness
the soul is the body's guest.
A day is going to come when
like a bird, it flies out of the cage.

The poor sons of Adam have sown
their seeds across the earth.
Some grew and some were lost.
My insides burn in this world,
my essence is afire. Some die young,
cut down like wheat still green.

If you visit the sick
or bring someone water,
tomorrow you'll be served
the wine of Truth.
If you give your clothes
to the poor, tomorrow
you'll be wearing astral clothes.
Yunus Emre, they say only two people
stay in this world forever—
Khidr and Elias, who drink the water of life.

52.

Oh Holy One, if ever You should ask—
these would be my answers to You:

I have sinned against myself,
but what, oh King, have I done to You?

Before I came, You said my soil was bad.
Before I was born, Adam rebelled.

In the eternal past I was written down a rebel.
You filled the universe with my loud voice.

You did whatever You wanted with me.
You brought me to whatever I found.

Have I constructed You? It's You who made me.
Why, oh Enricher, did You fill me with things to be
        ashamed of?

I open my eyes and what I see is the prison inside.
It's filled with animal needs, demons, and ambitions.

So that I would not die in this prison,
I have eaten unclean foods once or twice.

Has anything that You possess diminished,
or has my judgment ever surpassed Yours?

Did I eat Your daily bread and leave You hungry?
Did I waste Your wealth and leave You in poverty?

You stretch a bridge thin as a hair
and say, "Come and save yourself from My trap!"

Your servants build bridges with good in mind—
the good of crossing safely.
They build them strong so that people who pass over
might say, "This is a good bridge."

You set up scales to weigh people's intentions,
and You intend to put me in the fire.

It's grocers who need scales—
and greedy peddlars and druggists.

Because sin is the prize of the filthy,
even the useless gain something from Your being.

All I want from You is Your love.
Why uncover my faults and put them on a scale?

Will it please You to watch me burn?
For God's sake, oh Teacher of Creation, it's impossible.

You are All-Seeing. You, Yourself, know my state.
Why then do You need to weigh my actions?

Didn't Your need for revenge end when You killed me?
You made me rot and stuffed my eyes with dirt.

Has the hand of Yunus ever hurt You,
You who know the Seen and the Unseen?

So many empty words from a handful of dirt!
What do You need, oh Generous One, oh Power!

TURKISH FIRST LINES:

The Roman numeral references refer to: Gölpinarli, Abdülbâki.
Yunus Emre, Hayati ve Bütün Siirleri. Istanbul 1981, except
where otherwise stated.

1. Whoever is given the dervish path
Her kime kim dervishlik bagishlana
CCLXXXII

2. If I told you about a land of love
X (Eyüboglu Collection)

3. Ask those who know,
Bilenlere sormak gerek bu tendeki can neyimish?
XXI

4. We entered the house of realization,
Manî evine daldik vücud seyrini kildik
CCXXII

5. The drink sent down from Truth,
Hak'tan inen sherbeti içtik elhamdü lillah
CXIV

6. Let's say the name of Allah all the time.
Allah diyelim daim, Mevlâm görelim neyler
CXIII (Eyüboglu Collection)

7. The mature ones are a sea.
Erenler bir denizdir âshik gerek dalasi
CCLII

8. Our laws are different from other laws.
CXLV (Eyüboglu Collection)

9. Let the deaf listen to the mute.
Dilsizler haberini kulaksiz dinleyesi
CCXCVII

10. I haven't come here to settle down.
Benim bunda kararim yok ben bunda gitmege geldim
CCLXIX

11. A single word can brighten the face
Keleci bilen kishinin yüzünü agede bir söz
CLXXVII

II.

13. To be in love with love is to gain a soul,
Eger aski seversen cân olâsin
CCLXXIX

14. True speech is the fruit of not speaking.
Söylememek harcisi söylemegin hasidir
CIV

15. Leave appearances. Come to essence and meaning.
Suretten gel sifâta onda ma'ni bulasin
CXC

16. That by which our hearts are held,
XL (Eyüboglu Collection)

17. Oh Friend, when I began to love You,
Ey dost seni sevelden aklim gitti kaldim ben
XCI

18.How strange I feel under the hand of this love.
Acep oldu halim bu ashk elinden
LXXXVI

19. What sweet news of love shall I deliver
Ashiklara ne diyem ashk haberinden shirin
XCII

20. Beloved, Your love pierces stone.
Dost senin ashkin oku key kati tashtan geçer
LXXVI

21. My soul, the way of the masters
Canim erenler yolu inceden inceyimish
CLXXX

22. Hey friends, whoever swore off love?
Ey yarenler kim ishitti âshik tovbe kildigini
CIII

23. Do you know, my friends, where the real saints are?
Bilir misiz ey yarenler gercek erenler kandadir
LXXII

24. I wasn't sober until I drank the wine of Love.
Aklim bashima gelmedi ashk sharabin tatmayinca
CXIII

25. The moment this sweetheart caught my eye
Kaçan ol dilber benim gözüme tudash oldu
XCVI

III.

26. Wisdom comes from knowing wisdom.
Ilim ilim bilmektir ilim kendin bilmektir
CLXXVI

27. If you've broken a single heart,
XL (Eyüboglu Collection)

28. Those who became complete
Hakiyatin ma'nîsin sherh ile bilmediler
CVII

29. I am a sufi in the eyes of the people.
Sufiyim halk içinde tesbih elimden gitmez
CCXLVI

30. Before you're able to give your soul
Sen canindan geçemeden cânan arzu kilarsin
CCV

32. Don't advise those who aren't in love.
LXXXIII (Eyüboglu Collection)

33. Those who learned to be truly human
CCXXXVII (Eyüboglu Collection)

IV.

34. Whatever I say, You are the subject.
Ne söz keleci der isem dilim seni söyleyecek
LV

35. Soul of my soul, without You I have no work to do.
Sensin benim cânim cani sensiz karârim yokdurur
XLVIII

36. I am a fatherless pearl unrecognized by the sea.
Bir dürr-i yetimem ki görmedi beni umman
CLVIII

37. My love for you goes deeper than my soul
Severim ben seni candan içeri
CXXV

38. I have found the soul of souls.
CLXXVI (Eyüboglu Collection)

39. I am before and I am after
CCLXI (Eyüboglu Collection)

40. Love is my sect and religion.
Ey âshiklar ey âshiklar mezhep ü din asktir bana
LXVII

41. Truth gave me a heart bewildered
Hak bir gönül verdi banâ hâ demeden hayrân olur
CXXII

42. The rivers of paradise flow, chanting Allah, Allah
Sholjenettin irmaklari

43. The inner man knows no worries on this path.
Ma'ni eri bu yolda melül olasi degil
XXIII

44. One day I had taken a walk
XI (Eyüboglu Collection)

45. Truth fills the world,
Hak cihâna doludur kimsene Kakk'i bilmez
CCLXI

46. Oh disciple of love, open your eyes,
Ey ashk eri aç gözünü yer yüzüne eyle nazar
XVII

47. If you need to be warned, come look at these graves.
Sana ibret gerek ise gel göresin bu sinleri
IV

48. Put the world and its adornments aside,
Kogil dünyâ bezegini bu dünya yeldir ya hayâl
CCLXIV

49. Whatever separates you from the Truth
Seni Hak'tan yigani her neyise ver gider
XVIII

50. This King, He keeps on doing His work.
Ey pâdishah ey pâdishah her dem için düzedurur
XXV

51. My life came and went like the wind,
Geldi geçti ömrüm benim shol yel esip geçmish gibi
VII

52. Oh Holy One, if ever You should ask—
Ya ilahi ger sual etsen bana
CCLIII

Refik Algan, M.D. lives in Istanbul, Turkey and is a student of the Sufi path.

Kabir Edmund Helminski lives in Vermont and is the Director of the Threshold Society which seeks to apply traditional spiritual teachings to contemporary life. He is also the author/translator of *The Ruins of The Heart, Selected Lyric Poetry of Jelaluddin Rumi.*